Mary

and her Bible

Dear Reader,

We hope you enjoy the famous traditional story of Mary Jones.

With all stories like this some of the facts are uncertain, and recently discovered records suggest that Mary's father may have died when she was quite young.

Because we don't have Mary's diaries, many things in the story may have happened quite differently. However, we do have records of the first meetings of the British and Foreign Bible Society so we do know how things worked out in the end.

Published by Bible Society

Worldwide co-edition organized
and produced by
Lion Hudson plc
Wilkinson House, Jordan Hill Road,
Oxford OX2 8DR, England
www.lionhudson.com

ISBN 987-0-564-04567-9

This Edition 2017
First UK edition published in1992 by
The British and Foreign Bible Society
Stonehill Green
Westlea
Swindon SN5 7DG

A catalogue record for this book is available from the British Library

Printed and bound in Malaysia
2017

Mary Jones and her Bible

BY MIG HOLDER
Illustrated by Tony Morris

Deep in the Welsh hills perched a neat greystone cottage surrounded by a patchwork garden of vegetables and flowers: green cabbages and orange marigolds, scarlet runner-bean flowers and purple clumps of herbs. The wooden shutters at each window, fastened in winter to keep out the icy winds, were flung open. The front door was open too, and summer sunshine poured onto the scrubbed stone floor of the porch. Everything looked calm and bright.

Everything, that is, except the little girl who suddenly catapulted out of the open doorway. You could see at once that she was in a bad mood. She stamped her foot and shouted something back into the cottage. Then, with a scowling face, she marched off behind the house, reappearing moments later holding up the corners of her white apron. Reaching into the apron, she drew out a handful of something and flung it on the ground.

'Here you are, you stupid pecky things!' she shouted.

At once a dozen chickens appeared, scratching their way out of the bushes. Flinging out the corners of her apron, the girl emptied the rest of the grain over the hens in a flurry.

'I hate you, I hate you, I hate you,' she muttered as the grain fell to the ground. Then she flounced off to the furthest corner of the garden and threw herself down under an apple tree.

The girl's name was Mary, and she lived about two hundred years ago on the very edge of a little Welsh village. Her family was quite poor, so she and her mother and father had to work very hard to make a living. Her father, Mr Jones, was a weaver. He would sit at his loom in the back room of the cottage all the daylight hours, whizzing the shuttle back and forth, to make cloth to sell at market or to the richer people round about.

Mary knew how hard he worked – and she did try to be helpful. But sometimes she just felt so miserable.

'It's so boring!' she would say to herself, angrily tearing up handfuls of grass. 'Everyday is the same as the one before.'

Mary couldn't read or write, and there was no school for her to go to. So every day she had to help her mother clean the house and look after the garden. Every day they baked bread and stirred the stew. Every evening they mended and patched their clothes. Every day Mary fed the hens. Every night she carefully locked them all up in the henhouse, for fear of foxes.

Mostly Mary was happy; but sometimes she got tired of doing the same job over and over again – weeding the cabbage patch, when it seemed only a day since she had last done it! She would stand in the garden and look down the valley, wishing she had a friend to play with. For the Jones family rarely saw anyone else; their nearest neighbour was half a mile away.

But Sunday was their rest day. The big loom was silent, the house was spick and span, and Mary and her mother baked enough bread on Saturday to last over till Monday. On Sunday morning whatever the weather, the family set off over the hill to chapel.

It was two miles to the village, but Mary was used to walking and knew each step brought her nearer to her few friends – children of the other families who lived in the valley. They shouted and waved to each other outside the chapel, exchanging news at the top of their voices, until, all too soon, the grown-ups told them to quieten down and go into the meeting.

The service was always very long. Mary liked singing the hymns, but her heart would sink when the minister stood up to begin his sermon. His voice seemed to drone on for hours, and it was so difficult to understand what he was saying. The wooden pew seemed to get harder and harder, and it was all Mary could do not to fidget. If she did, her father would tap her on the knee and look sternly at her. To try to pass the time, Mary would count the cobwebs high up in the chapel ceiling, or make out shapes in the shadows cast by the chapel lamps.

Sometimes, when the minister was reading from the huge black Bible, she would try to imagine what it would be like to be able to read. Mary had once crept to the front of the chapel after service and stood on tiptoe to peer at the strange black squiggles running across the page. She couldn't understand how anyone could make head or tail of them and would never get the chance!

But then suddenly, one Sunday, the minister said: 'I have a very special announcement.' He cleared his throat importantly. 'We are to have a school in the village. All children may attend. The new school will open next week.'

Mary could hardly believe what she heard!

But it was true. A special teacher was to come and set up a school in the chapel building for three whole months. Not only would Mary have the chance to learn to read and write – she would also see her friends every day! She couldn't wait! The days seemed to pass even more slowly than usual, and the jobs her mother asked her to do seemed even more boring.

When the day came for Mary to start school, she was so excited that she woke up while it was still dark. She lay staring out of her bedroom window at the black sky. She wondered what it would be like to read, to decipher the strange marks that held the secret of stories, of people and places she couldn't have imagined. Then suddenly she was afraid. Suppose it was too hard? Suppose she couldn't do it and the others laughed at her? Along with her excitement, she felt a tight knot of worry in her stomach.

So Mary was glad when dawn at last crept slowly over the hills. She jumped out of bed, quickly put on the clean clothes she had laid out the night before, and crept downstairs. She cut some bread and cheese for lunch and wrapped it carefully in a square cloth. Then she woke her parents, said goodbye to them, and set off to walk the two miles to school.

When she arrived, most of the other children were already waiting excitedly outside the chapel. At last Mr Ellis, the teacher, opened the door. They all filed in and sat down. The children were all together in

one class, whether they were six or thirteen, because none of them had ever been to school before.

Mr Ellis handed out slates and sticks of chalk, and showed them how to draw letter shapes. The chalk made a horrible squeaky noise on the slate, but Mary scarcely noticed, concentrating hard, poking out the tip of her tongue with the effort. She had never enjoyed herself so much!

As the days passed, Mr Ellis began writing complete words on the blackboard. As soon as a child could read these words, they could go to the front of the chapel and try to read from the single book there – the only book Mary had ever seen – the big Bible that the minister read from on Sundays.

Mary learned quickly, and could soon read a whole page at a time. She loved reading the stories of Jesus and the long-ago adventures of people such as Noah and Jonah. One day, on the long walk home from school, Mary found herself wondering what it would be like to have a book of her own.

Suddenly she had an idea! She rushed home and burst in on her parents.

'I've decided. I'm going to save up for a Bible of my own!'

There was no answer. She looked at her mother and father. Instead of being pleased, they seemed worried.

'But books are so expensive,' said her mother at last. 'More than people like us can afford. I wouldn't want you to be disappointed.'

'Don't you start getting above yourself now, girl,' added her father.

Mary was upset.

'I *will* do it!' she shouted. 'If I have to save up for twenty years. Anyway, I *can read*. You wait till next Sunday; you'll see!'

She burst into tears and marched up to her bedroom. Her parents looked miserably at each other.

Later that evening, Mary's father went to his workshop, and, by the light of a candle, made a strong wooden box. When it was finished, he hid it under his workbench.

What a surprise for Mary's mother and father at chapel next Sunday! The minister announced: 'Our lesson this morning will be read by Mary Jones.'

With pink cheeks and pounding heart, Mary stood up and walked to the lectern. She carefully turned over the pages of the great book till she came to the place that Mr Ellis had marked for her. Then she took a deep breath and started to read. At first her voice was a bit shaky, but it soon became louder and stronger as she read in Welsh:

'Jesus said "Everyone who comes to me and hears what I say and acts upon it – I will show you what he is like. He is like a man who, building his house, dug deep and laid the foundations on rock. When the flood came, the river burst upon that house, but could not shift it, because it had been soundly built."'

When she had finished, Mary hurried back to her place. She shot a sideways look at her parents, who were beaming with pride. After the service, all sorts of people came up to Mary to congratulate her on learning to read so quickly.

'You must be so proud of her,' Mrs Evans from the big farm said to Mary's mother.

'Well, yes, we are,' said her mother. 'But she has this grand idea of saving up to buy a Welsh Bible of her own.'

'And so she shall!' cried Mrs Evans. 'A girl with the determination to learn to read so quickly will surely succeed at anything she puts her mind to. In the meantime, she must come and practise reading our Bible at the farmhouse.'

So the very next Saturday found Mary knocking a bit nervously on the big front door of the Evans' farmhouse. It was a much grander house than Mary's. It had lots of windows at the front, and a huge yard.

Mrs Evans showed Mary into a room with heavy, dark furniture and lace table-cloths. There wasn't just one, but a whole row of books lined up on a shelf. Mary wondered what they could all be. Mrs Evans lifted down the Bible and pulled up a chair for Mary.

'Take as long as you like, dear,' she said. 'Then come to the kitchen for a drink before you leave.'

Mary turned the pages carefully. She started with the chapters they had learned in school, running her finger under the words as she read. Then she turned to the very front of the Bible and read the story of how the world began. She tried to remember everything she read, so that she could repeat it to her parents when she got home.

After a while, it began to get dark. Mary did not like to ask Mrs Evans for a candle. So she lifted the Bible carefully back into its space on the shelf and found her way to the kitchen. Mrs Evans was baking at an enormous scrubbed table. She smiled and passed Mary a cup of milk and a warm welshcake.

'Come whenever you like,' she said.

'Thank you very much,' said Mary, and then added shyly: 'What I'd really like to do is save up for a Bible of my own.'

Mrs Evans smiled again. 'I think you'll find your mother and father will help,' she said.

Back home, Mary took off her cloak and hung it on the peg. As she turned back into the room, her father held something out towards her.

'We know how much you want a Bible,' he said. 'We'll do all we can to help you. Here's a money-box to keep your savings in.' He handed her the wooden box he had hidden under his workbench.

'You can have two chickens of your own, and sell their eggs,' said her mother.

'And one of my hives shall be yours, so that you can sell the honey from the bees,' added her father.

'Oh, thank you, thank you.' Mary hugged them. 'I'll work and work until I get my Bible.'

And that is exactly what she did.

Children in those days didn't get pocket-money, so Mary had to find ways of earning the money, while still doing all her chores in the house. When there was any wool left over from her mother's knitting, Mary begged it to knit brightly-coloured socks that she could sell at the market. And when harvest-time came round, though she was very young, Mary went to work for nearby farmers, helping tie and stack the bundles of grain. But it was exhausting work, and she was paid only a few pennies a day.

The pile of coins in Mary's money-box seemed to grow so slowly. Quite often she was tempted to give up and spend the money on a pretty dress or a new pair of shoes. But then she would remind herself that every extra penny in the box brought her nearer to having the Bible she dreamed of.

Six whole years passed. Six long winters and six harvests. Mary saw six birthdays and six Christmases go by. She was now quite grown-up – fifteen years old! But in all that time, however busy she was, Mary never let go of her resolve one day to own a Bible of her very own.

Then, one winter's evening, she took down the box from the mantelpiece and tipped her pile of coins out onto the table. She counted and then counted again, just to be sure.

'Mother, father, guess what! I'm almost there! Only a few pence more, and I shall have enough money to buy my Bible! I can't wait for Sunday – I'll ask the minister how to get one. Then, as soon as I've saved that last bit, I'll be ready.'

But Mary was in for a surprise. After chapel, she waited patiently for a chance to speak to the minister.

'Mr Hugh,' she began. 'You know that I've been saving up for a Bible...'.

Mr Hugh held up his hand. '...A little bird told me that you have almost enough money now. Some of us in the village have taken a small collection to make up the amount you need.'

He pressed a little bag of coins into her hand.

Mary was overwhelmed. She knew that most of the village people could not really afford to give away any of their money.

'Please, please thank them all for me,' she said. 'Now – tell me where I have to go to get my Bible.' Mr Hugh looked serious now.

'Mary,' he said. 'The nearest place is Bala, and that is twenty-five miles away. Thirteen times as far as you walk to chapel!'

'I'm used to walking,' said Mary simply.

Mr Hugh hesitated.

'But Mary, suppose when you arrive, there are no Bibles left?'

Mary turned smiling eyes up to his.

'I know there will be,' she said.

Mr Hugh returned her smile, but, inside, he wondered.

Mary's parents knew that, after she had been saving for so long, there was no way they would stop her going on her long journey. So, very early one morning, they hugged her and waved her off, praying that God would look after her.

In her hand Mary held a knotted cloth full of bread and cheese to eat on the way. In her pocket was a purse full of the money she had saved. Over her shoulder hung a special leather bag which she had sewn to bring back her precious Bible in. And in her head she carried a name and address that the minister had given her. He had a friend who lived in Bala, and had told Mary that as soon as she arrived, she was to find Mr Edwards' house, and he would be sure to help her.

At first it was easy. Mary knew all the paths near her own village. It was a bright, sunny day, and she stepped out lightly, humming as she went. Now and then she passed someone at a cottage window, or people working in the fields, and she called out: 'Hello!' But she didn't stop. She knew she had a very long way to go.

When the sun was high in the sky, she guessed it was about midday. She sat down by a stream to rest, drank some of the clear water, and rinsed her aching feet. She ate most of the bread and cheese, carefully saving some in case she needed it later.

After lunch, Mary set off again, but now the way seemed harder. The hill-paths seemed steeper, the ground stonier, and the sun even hotter than before. For the first time Mary began to wonder whether she would make it. She had already been walking for seven hours, and there was still a long way to go.

Then an awful thought struck her, sending a sick feeling to the pit of her stomach: supposing there was no Bible to be had? What if the few Bibles printed in her own language, Welsh, had all gone? Trying to push this thought to the back of her mind, Mary trudged on. But her legs were stiff and tired, and more than once she stumbled on the stony path, tears springing to her eyes from pain and exhaustion.

In front of her the path divided. Which way should she take? There was no time for mistakes, if she was to get to Bala before dark. Mary was afraid. She tried hard to recall the directions her father had given her. Then she chose the winding path that led up a wooded hill. When she rested on the stile at the top, she looked down and saw at last, to her delight, the town of Bala spread out before her.

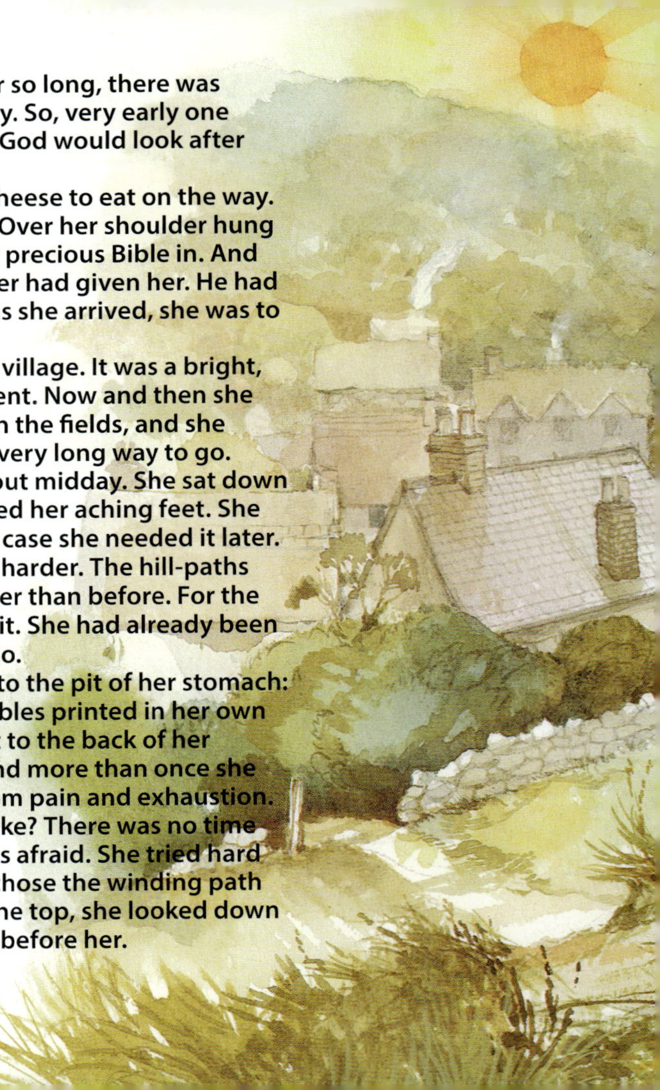

From somewhere Mary seemed to find new energy. She practically flew down the grassy hillside to the edge of the town, and it seemed no time at all before she found her way to the house where Mr Edwards lived. As the door swung open, she suddenly felt shy. Her words came out all in a rush.

'Please sir, the minister at Abergynolwyn said you are a friend of his – my name is Mary Jones – and I have been saving up for six years to buy a Bible – and he said...'

'Hold on a minute,' said a gentle voice. 'Come inside and tell me from the beginning.'

Mary looked up into the kind face of Mr Edwards and then followed him into the house. When he had heard all of Mary's story, he was quite amazed.

'And you walked twenty-five miles just today?' he asked. Mary nodded. She was suddenly so tired she could barely stand up.

'Then first you need a meal and a good night's sleep. Tomorrow we shall see about getting your Bible.'

Mr Edwards' maid led Mary away to the kitchen for a good dinner, and then tucked her up in a huge soft bed covered with a patchwork quilt. As her head touched the white pillow, Mary fell straight to sleep, dreaming of what tomorrow would bring.

Next morning Mr Edwards explained that they would need to call on a Mr Charles, who had received a parcel of Welsh Bibles from London, and would be able to sell one to Mary.

'I just hope he has some left,' said Mr Edwards under his breath, as they hurried through the narrow streets.

'You're very lucky,' smiled Mr Charles when they explained why they had come. 'This is the very last one.'

He took out a beautifully-bound brand-new Bible and passed it to Mary. She took it in both hands and stared at it for a long moment. Her own Bible at last! She could hardly believe it. Then she gave Mr Charles her purse full of money, and tucked the Bible safely into her leather bag.

'Read it carefully and learn from it,' said Mr Charles as he waved goodbye.

'I will – and thank you!' called Mary, hurrying off up the street.

The journey home seemed so much shorter than the day before. Mary sped over the hillsides, clasping her leather bag. But she was very tired by the time she saw the lamplights of her own village in the distance. Her mother and father and all her friends were waiting at the edge of the village.

Mary held the Bible high above her head. 'I got it! I got it!' she shouted. And to herself she added, 'Now at last I can read my own Bible in my own language.'

Long after Mary had left for home, Mr Charles sat in his study thinking about the girl who had saved for so long and walked so far to get a Welsh Bible of her own. Bibles in Welsh were in very short supply, and, even when they could be found, they were much too expensive for ordinary people to afford. Mr Charles made up his mind to do something about it.

And so a few months later, at a great meeting of important men and women in London, Mr Charles climbed onto the platform and said: 'Ladies and gentlemen, I would like to tell you a true story about a little girl called Mary Jones...'

And all the people listened spellbound as he described how Mary had patiently saved her money and walked all the way to Bala to get the Bible she had dreamed of. When he had finished there was silence. Then suddenly people were scrambling to their feet.

'We must print more Welsh Bibles,' cried one.

'And make them cheaper,' shouted someone else.

And from a loud voice at the back: 'Why not Bibles in every language?'

So, there and then, a society was formed to make Bibles in every language for people all over the world.

Mr Charles would never have imagined that today, two hundred years later, that same organisation would still be at work. It is called the British and Foreign Bible Society. Together with Bible Societies in many other countries, it has translated the Bible into almost two thousand languages. So today almost anyone who wants to can now buy a Bible in their own language - without having to save for so long, or walk so far, as Mary Jones.

Across the world, millions of people are not engaging with the Bible. This is often because the Scriptures aren't available or accessible, or because their significance and value haven't yet been recognised. Working in over 200 countries, Bible Society is a charity and on a global mission to offer the Bible to every man, woman and child. This is because we believe that when people engage with the Bible, lives can be changed, for good.